Then The Unexpected Happened

By

Katrina A. McCain

Copyright © 2021 Katrina A. McCain

All rights reserved. No part of this book may be reproduced or used in any manner without the written permission of the author except for the use of quotations in a book review.

Poet Katrina McCain
PO Box 5211
Greensboro, NC 27435

Cover & Design Layout:
Carlos V. Kaigler /C'vaughn'K Graphic Designs/ The Poet B.GKL

Proofreader:
Dr. Patricia Demps, PhD.,D.D.

ISBN: 978-1-7379392-0-7

Then The Unexpected Happened

Katrina A. McCain

A COLLECTION OF POEMS

"Everything in the universe has a rhythm, everything dances."

~Maya Angelou~

Dedication

This book is dedicated to the best parts of me…

**Arrius Lavey McCain
&
Angela LeAnn McCain**

Table of Contents

Then The Unexpected Happened	
Dedication	
Table of Contents	
Foreword	I
Preface	III
Acknowledgments	V
Introduction	1
Words	3
Chapter I: Loving Without Limits	**5**
Humbled Spirit	6
My First Love	7
Because She Decided to Love	9
Word Whore	10
Balancing and Thumping	11
Poetic Crush	12
Perfect Storm	13
Naked	14
Love Letter to Younger Katrina	15
Intimacy	17
Me Meeting Me	18
Addicted	20

Fantasy vs Reality   21
Yourself   23

Chapter II: Heartbroken   25

Claps   26
As We Say Goodbye   27
Dear Big Sis   28
Ignite   30
Chocolate Covered Excuses   31
Mistakes   32
Poison in My Belly   34
Love Songs in the Rain   36
Obligations and Situations   38
Does Love?   40
Can You?   41
Give Back... You Didn't   42
Loving You from Over Here   44
Changes   46
Stuck Between Two Loves   47
Grandma   49

Chapter III: Socially Conscious   51

Mask   52
Hands Up   53
Generational Thinking   54
The House on Main Street   56
War Cry   58
Where, When What Happened?   60

Comparisons and Confusion	62
A Good Friend But a Bad Girl	63
I Didn't Want to Die That Day	64
FREE	66
Chapter IV: Inspired by God	**67**
Sweet Life	68
What Are You Trying to Tell Me?	69
Dear God	70
I Found Her	71
Garden of Despair	72
Pride	74
Favor	76
Recommitted	77
Blessings	79
About the Author	81
Follow Katrina A. McCain	83
Other Books	85
Upcoming Projects	87
Fragile Love with Glass Affections	88
Guard	98

Foreword

I have the pleasure of writing the foreword for this book and I count it an honor. I witnessed firsthand Katrina's work ethics and her solid discipline, which helped shape my career as an Educator. Her principals and morals set her apart from the crowd. I couldn't think of a better way to further describe Katrina other than creating her favorite form of writing, poetry.

A Chip Off the Old Block

Endless nights filled with grind and grit
Dreams unfolding with bountiful bliss
Time invested and passions unraveled
Stories of the many experiences you've traveled
Your opinions stain the paper in black hue
Every valley you entered, you passed right through
Observing and taking notes with a scholar's desire
You will never know the number of souls you inspire
From struggle to triumph, I witnessed firsthand
Any doubt that existed will no longer stand
Your legacy of literacy is cemented in stone
My admiration and your success have graciously grown
As I draw to a close, know one thing is for sure
You have impacted our lives and so many more

It has been great watching Katrina's journey on completing her second book of poetry and her writing career soaring to the next level. I have seen all kinds of emotions from her while writing. I am a smart man, and I know to leave her alone unless she asks for my help with proofreading or bouncing ideas around.

Finally, thank you Katrina, Mom Dukes, for everything you do and the example you live. My daughter and I appreciate you and we love you. Congratulations on completing Book 2!

Arrius L. McCain
Greensboro, NC
9/1/2021

Preface

I wrote this poetry book as a way to release intimate feelings I have experienced through love and the aftermath of love. Love is so unpredictable, but love is so enjoyable and amazing. I believe love is the most powerful and most beautiful thing for us to experience in this world. Even after a heartbreak, love can be achieved if one is willing to open himself/herself up to the possibility of being loved again. Past hurt hinders people from opening up to love because the consequence of love is outside of one's control.

My personal feelings about love, my belief in love, and my hope for better days because of love are the very reasons I am able to breathe life in the upcoming pages for you to feel and enjoy. My words float from the pages of each poem to reveal my vulnerability and sensitivity to matters meaning the most to the world and me. My hope is you will connect to the emotions captured in each poem, even if you disagree with the subject matter. While reading the poems, try to think about your own personal beliefs from a different perspective.

This poetry book is important because of the lessons the world should have learned in 2020 and 2021, while living in the midst of a global pandemic and the height of the Black Lives Matter Movement. While the lessons I learned may be different from someone else's lessons learned, we all walked away slightly different people. My poetry bridges the gap between people of different races and different political issues by showing them it is not necessary to choose sides in all matters. By doing so, the entire world is hurting as a consequence. Unity and love will solve most of the issues we are experiencing in the world as a whole.

I delicately described sensitive situations, with as much love as I possibly could. You will have the opportunity to peak into someone else's life, who live drastically different from you, and witness their struggles firsthand. With love, the proper respect, and a clear understanding; an opened minded person's entire perspective on life could change after reading this book. Changed perspectives change communities, the nation, and the world by making living conditions better for all people regardless the color of skin.

Acknowledgments

I humbly thank God for the successful completion of this project. Numerous obstacles presented themselves over the two years of writing this book, and those roadblocks were enough to delay the process altogether. However, God always provided a quiet space, a motivated mind, and fresh ideas. I also thank God for who he is in my life, and the love he has for me on my highest of days and my lowest of days.

To my Son... Thank you for being more than a son! There isn't enough space in this section or the entire book to express my gratitude for all you do. Thanks for being my proofreader and contributor of ideas to this project. You were patient in moments I was not so patient, and your calmness definitely stilled the waters. Your endless support and love mean the world to me! Keep striving for greatness and making me proud of you in the process.

To my precious Granddaughter... Thank you Pumpkin Boo for looking at me through eyes of admiration as you encourage me to be my very best. You kept me company in my work station while I was working on poems and the crayon marks you contributed to the poems were the best parts. You brought joy to my writing on nights I was tired and wanted to quit. Those crayon marks reminded me of the legacy I am leaving for you and quitting is never an option.

To my Mom... Thank you Mommy for checking on the progress of my book from the first day to the last day. You called often to ask how many poems I completed. Your inquiring made me grind even harder. Many times, I fell behind on deadlines I set, and your phone calls held me accountable to finish this project on time. You are the reason this book is coming out on time. Thank you for pushing me when you did not know you were doing so. I just want to make you proud, and I pray I have done so.

To my amazing Sisters… Thank you for demonstrating strength and determination in all you have endured the last couple of years. Life has hit you with some mighty powerful blows and you kept on keeping on. Thank you for being my sounding boards and my shoulders to cry on in my difficult times. The safe spaces you provided were truly valued and not taken for granted. The strength, the motivation, and inspiration I felt after one of our talks was exactly what I needed to keep going on during difficult times. Thanks for being my light during some very dark times.

To my Nieces and Nephews… Thank you for being my inspiration by simply living your lives the way you do. I watched you grow into the beautiful people you are, and I beam with joy after every conversation or every picture I see of you. Your accomplishments such as your marriages, your children, and your career choices make your Auntie super proud. I try to be a positive influence in your lives by grinding harder, working with integrity in all things, and presenting the best version of me to the world and you.

To my Friends… Thank you for 15 - 40 precious years of friendship from some of you guys, and the memories we have together are stored in my heart forever. You provide positive breaks in my life with laugher and love in moments I needed it the most. You never passed judgement on my situations. You always made me feel comfortable enough to share my most intimate thoughts. You never made me feel ashamed for my mistakes. Knowing I can count and depend on you means everything to me.

To the memory of my Dad… Thank you for leading by example and being a positive influence in my life. The lessons you taught shaped the woman I am today. Losing you twenty-eight years ago was so traumatic and still painful today. Your death forced me to become a stronger and more independent person. I try to make you proud of me in all things I do. I think of you always. Your famous words, "Guess who loves you baby", still ring in my ear and I love you Baby!

To the memory of my Stepdad.... Thank you for the countless sacrifices you made for our family. You led by example on what it looks like for a real man to take care of a woman, and her children. I heard you loud and clear when you preached not to settle on anyone or anything, and I could do bad all by myself. I am eternally grateful for being treated like your daughter instead of your stepdaughter, and your memory lives on forever in our hearts.

Introduction

I wrote this poetry book because it felt so good after releasing my first poetry book, "**Because She Decided To Love.**" The responses from people were mind blowing and motivated me to continue to write. Now, I have actually been called a "Love Expert;" when I still do not know the magic formula to making love work. However, I believe love is as beautiful as poetry, and they complement each other so well. I know this to be true because I blindly chase after love and poetry every day. I personally cannot live without poetry, like the world cannot live nor heal without love.

After releasing my first poetry book, "**Because She Decided To Love**," I continued to write poems straight from my heart. However, this book took a different turn than originally planned. I no longer wrote poems with the beautiful fluff like before, which are the poems I enjoy writing the most. Instead, some poems in this poetry book come with layers of depth, confusion, hurt, and pain from the aftermath of love.

Love is so enjoyable and so unpredictable. Love makes the world a brighter place as it fights against hate and racism every day. I became more socially conscious during 2020-2021 while experiencing the Black Live Matters and the Corona Virus Pandemic. The world became divided and forced people to make decisions on critical matters by political views, which only caused more chaos. I wrote several poems highlighting the issues brought to the forefront in my powerful Social Issue Section titled, "Socially Conscious." I do not expect agreement on the subject matter of every poem, but the emotions in each poem should affect every heart the same.

While taking a walk through my Love Section titled, "Loving Without Limits," and my Religious Section titled, "Inspired by God," I ask you to relax in love. Inhale the beauty of love into your lungs and exhale anything exhibiting hate. I included poems in both sections to demonstrate, even after a heartbreak, love is possible. One has to choose to love whole-heartedly, instead of remaining in their protected space to make love work.

Because She Decided to Love… Then The Unexpected Happened! Unfortunately, some of those unexpected times result in painful heartbreaks. In my heartbreak section, titled, "Heartbroken," you will see my exposed heart, and how I dealt with the pain from my personal heartbreaks. I was vulnerable as I shared how confusion, hurt, pain, and forgiveness can be difficult journeys to recovery. I show you if you heal properly from a heartbreak, new possibilities of love are beyond the horizon.

I would like for you to feel my heart in each and every poem as I tackle sensitive topics in this poetry book. I wrote the poems as delicately as I could. However, some topics cannot be written without blatantly stating how I felt about the subject matter. I expressed my personal feelings and emotions on experiences I encountered and the experiences of others. I would like for you to read the poem in its entirety, before passing judgement on the subject matters.

Please take another roller coaster ride with me, after the bumpy one experienced in **"Because She Decided to Love."** If you are still a little shaky from the previous ride, I highly suggest you tightly and securely buckle yourself in place before turning the next pages of **"Then The Unexpected Happened."**

Words

Words flow smoothly over an invisible beat turning itself into a beautiful work of art.

Chapter I:
Loving Without Limits

Humbled Spirit

Admiration, love, and respect do not need to be chased down or sought out; as they will find your humbled spirit hiding behind your work.

My First Love

I remember the first time I met you
    12 years old with glasses and no confidence.
I really did not think you were interested in me.
I saw how you played with others in class.
You were in all the love letters passed under the desks.
I blushed every time you interacted with me though.
You always said the right things on days I needed a smile.
It was not long before I saw your seriousness in me.
Pretty quickly, I hung you in my locker with love.
I scribbled your name on all of my notebooks.
You made me nervous every time I thought about you.
You wanted to share our relationship with the world.
Too shy and not wanting criticism of my awkward life,
I cowardly ran from you without a goodbye.
I comfortably lived my life and became complacent.
I had many accomplishments without you.
However, I often thought of you over the years.
I would not dare try to rekindle our relationship.
I sensed your presence during rough times in my life.
Surely, you had settled with one who appreciated you.
Not knowing you were looking for me all these years,
I reluctantly and surprisingly answered your call one night.
I blushed and giggled like a teenage girl.
I recalled the first time we met and how you made me feel.
You were unsure of how I would accept you in my life again.
Night turned into day, and I still did not want to let you go.
I was scared of losing you a second time around.
Our reconnection was nothing less than remarkable.
Not caring how the world feels about us being together now,

We leave our love on everyone who hears our story.
You make me smile as you make my dreams come true.
Your love for me inspires me to do better and be better.
I vow to never leave you nor forsake you again.
My heart is the signed documentation of my commitment.
Without further ado and with all my love on this day,
I choose to spend the rest of my life with you, Poetry!

Because She Decided to Love

Because she decided to love,
She risked it all.
Unforeseen circumstances
Were not in her favor,
But she allowed love
To heal her from within.
Even after a heartbreak,
She still believed
Love is the most
Beautiful thing in the world.
There is no way
She could live
Without love!

Word Whore

Word Whoring is what I do.
    I list my services on all the websites,
Twitter, Facebook, and Instagram.
"I'm the best Word Whore in town."
I promise to make your fantasies come true,
As I vividly recite your wildest dreams
Between the lines of these sheets.
My reputation proceeds me.
I get a call to perform tonight.
I slip on my sexiest dress.
Spray on my best smelling perfume.
I greet my clients upon arrival.
I lick my lips and clear my throat.
Grabbing the mic with both hands,
I spit another perfect combination of words.
Word Whoring with everyone in the crowd.
No discrimination as I tease everyone's mind.
As I leave it all on the stage,
I enjoy the warmth of the aftermath.
My clients rush to the table for more of me.
Prepared with books of my Word Whoring,
I autograph every copy purchased with a kiss.
I gladly gather the money left on my table.
I swallow the last drop of euphoria.
I bid farewell to more satisfied customers,
Leaving with stacks of money in my purse,
It was another great night of word whoring.
Yeah... "I'm the best Word Whore" in town!

Balancing and Thumping

Love is the balance needed
    As the world turns on its axel,
Attempting to recreate hope
By rejuvenating happiness.
Balancing…
Thumping …
Love is the thump in your chest
When you close your eyes,
To feel what your heart
Has been brewing.
Balancing…
Thumping…

Poetic Crush

Wanting to see his face and hear his voice tonight,
    I logged on his social media with high expectations.
Hoping to find an indication of him going live,
I hungered for another intimate, poetic encounter with him.
Dancing with the lyrical notes left from his last live,
I glanced at my newly written poem inspired by him.
Confessing I had fallen in love with my Poetic Crush,
I tucked the truth beneath the words in another poem.
Talking with a southern drawl and having a northern swag,
I could not determine where my Poetic Crush reside.
Fighting my shyness and my computer screen's safety,
I relied heavily on my creativity to capture his attention.
Hiding behind cute hearts and seducing comments,
I imagined people responding to our greatest masterpiece.
Collaborating with the most talent poet ever,
I smiled at the endless possibilities we could make.
Breaking my thoughts as social media signals he was live,
I could not contain the excitement he aroused within me.
Breathing deeper than I was moments before,
I confessed my Poetic Crush was the dopiest in the game.
Concentrating on his smooth voice and his perfect smile,
I noticed the passion behind the way he spit his words.
Delivering his messages with the right amount of passion,
I panted for more of his style, his talent, and his rawness.
Noticing my Poetic Crush was done performing,
I slowly released a deep breath and closed my laptop.
Burning my pen and paper to capture fresh feelings for him,
I tossed the poem in the never to see pile by my Poetic Crush.

Perfect Storm

Your love reminds me
Of the perfect storm
Raging outside!

Naked

I wish to run naked in the rain.
Not the typical nakedness
Where my clothes are off,
And the rain drenches my body.
Instead, I want to experience
The freedom of nothing
Weighing me down
As rumors, lies, half-truths,
And hate come my way.
I understand as I expose
My nakedness in the rain,
People will begin to compare
My life and my decisions
Against the storms in their lives.
I am cool with people discovering
My weaknesses and my flaws.
As we all have them!
But please let my puddles speak for me,
While I am running naked in the rain.
When the rain stops,
Through my rays of sunshine
My heart will be revealed to the world.
As the sun holds its place in the sky,
My heart demonstrates,
Who I am,
Why I love so hard,
Why I am loyal,
And why I am faithful,
After I run naked in the rain.

Love Letter to Younger Katrina

Trust me now if you never trust me again.
I love you and care about your now and then.
This love letter addresses issues you will go through.
Some you will get right, but others you will have no clue.
Bruised and battered by others will leave you with scars.
Healing and forgiving are the secrets to shining like a star.
Questions of am I enough, am I worthy, or I am pretty,
Will have you wanting to join the unnoticeable committee.
I speak life into you and all your situations, my Love.
Trust the guidance and advice from the man up above.
Please do not fall victim to the feelings of despair.
Everything in time will have a moment to repair.
The weight of the world is not yours to carry.
The problems of your family, please do not marry.
Peer pressure walks with you every day.
Nothing is wrong with walking the path left astray.
Be proud of yourself as your heart remains pure.
Others will see its beauty once they mature.
Life will not always upset or disappoint you.
Life is full of joys and pleasures you can pursue.
The roughest valleys will develop your character.
Mountaintops will show things that really matter.
Lift your head high, believe in yourself, and smile often.
All those doubts and fears will begin to soften.
Search within for your own hopes and dreams.
Blind the world as your unique light beams.
Teenage years are the worst as your body changes.
Voices and attitudes will be different in all ranges.
You are the number one person in your life.

Please wait on him willing to make you his wife.
Early twenties will take your life by storm.
Thinking you are grown, and others should conform.
In these years, be careful of the decisions you make.
Knee-jerk decisions can cause years of heartbreak.
Establish yourself before making lifelong choices.
Trading your body is not good even for Rolls-Royces.
Represent yourself as the queen you are within.
My precious Love, I agree everybody has their own sin.
Do not measure your decisions against someone else's life.
Every step not as big as theirs, will cut like a knife.
There is no secret to successfully overcome or conquer.
You are winning as long as you do not turn into a monster.
Wake up every day with a purpose and a plan.
I promise everything you do in time will stand.

Intimacy

I never stay awake long enough
   To see if my heartbeat
Syncs with yours.
The moment your arms
Hold me, I fall into
A love-spell trance.
The comfort of your intimacy
Intensely rocks me to sleep.
Hues of reds, oranges, and blues
Allude to the colorful intimacy
I experience with you.

Me Meeting Me

Fortunate enough to meet Me as Me,
I was able to experience my own energy.
My eyes watch Me grip the door handle.
Instant admiration and intrigue,
Piqued my interest about Me.
Beauty runs through my veins,
As the sunlight follows Me to my table.
In the quiet, secluded coffee shop,
Me smiles at Me from across the room.
Intimidating Me just a little bit,
An electromagnetic wave beckons Me.
Deep breath in. Deep breath out.
Floating across the room with no control,
Standing breathless in front of Me now.
Me extends my hand anxiously to Me.
My touch with my touch rocks the building,
As Me remain stuck in the moment forever.
I sense hesitation from Me as we stare at each other,
Fearing Me will prematurely destroy our connection.
Musically smooth, enchanting conversation,
Wakes up the vibes from Me to Me.
Affecting the atmosphere outside,
Clouds begin to collide with one another,
Causing a rainstorm to break the sunlight,
As my energy holds Me captive at Table 3.
My smile freezes the rain in midair,
Stopping the traffic from flowing,
On a Tuesday afternoon in Rush Hour.

Experiencing my own energy as myself
Resulted in beautiful, mesmerizing chaos,
As the world struggled to handle Me Meeting Me.

Addicted

Addicted!
   Hooked to the creation of my poetry,
Filled with flawless tempos and flows.
Each word's heartbeat and vibe,
Choke the pulse and pace,
Hastening through my heart and veins.
Obsessed!
Strokes from my hooked pen,
Burst with potent blemishes,
Altering relationships in my life.
Causing the Alphabet Rehab
To fail me once again.
Craft still calling from the dark!
Overdosed!

Fantasy vs Reality

In our fantasy world starring you and me,
   Everything and everybody are blocked out.
Reality paused as our game night begun.
Our mission statement was understood...
Let's play until we were both satisfied.
I brought the games as instructed.
Arriving with minutes to spare.
You brought the rules for the fantasy,
Keeping them fresh as always.
Our game night was about to begin.
Hours passed as our conversation was mesmerizing.
Thoughts of our last game night were fresh in my mind.
You look at me with THAT look
And I know it's THAT time!
Reality had to wait a little while longer.
The night was amazing!
Game 1 had begun.
We both brought our competitive side.
Trash talking started on the phone hours before.
Your texts sent my mind into defense mode.
Strategies started to form on my drive to you.
You always set up the perfect offense though.
You know I like the other side of the ball.
Your hands tightly held the side of the game.
As my lead grew deeper and deeper.
Jerseys, cheers, applauses, and laughter
Flooded the room for hours from pure fun
Completely detached from reality now.

I ducked and dodged the rules,
As you sidestepped and darted my winnings
Respectfully and courteously as competitors.
Dice and board games were all over the floor.
Whew…. It was no holding back that night.
Game 2 and Game 3 were very intense.
No limits nor constraints in our fantasy world.
The clock slowly ended our fantasy night.
Reality signaled game night was over.
We agreed our fantasy world felt so good.
Lying on the couch with our feet propped up,
Resting arm in arm and hand in hand.
Reality vs fantasy forced me to say,
"It's time for me to head to bed for the night."
As I stood at the door, I said "But wait...
When are we going to have game night again?"

Yourself

The most important person in your life lies within the mirror. Love him/her as intensely as you love others.

Chapter II:
Heartbroken

Claps

Listen carefully to the silent claps, ringing the loudest in your presence.

As We Say Goodbye

Dedicated to the late
Christine Richardson Moody
(1956-2021)

Death has a way of leaving holes in our hearts.
    Grief blinds us and tells us we are worlds apart.
Uncontrollable tears flow and cloud our vision.
Broken heart pieces are floating around like ribbons.
Our minds catch glimpses of you smiling and dancing.
Your voice and laughter suddenly have us reminiscing.
You had your own special relationship with all of us.
Always a phone call away and your solid love was a plus.
Even in this moment, the gentleness of your love soothes.
The atmosphere of sorrow shifts and our sadness moves.
Words can't express how much we are missing you.
We take comfort in knowing you are happy and resting too.
On today, in the earthly realm, we say our final goodbyes.
One day, yours arms will hold us, and the same love will apply.

Dear Big Sis

Dear Big Sis,

I smiled today and I was actually happy.
I texted our family I loved them.
I was spotlighted on a podcast on social media.
The poem chosen was written for your nephew.
I was humbled, grateful, and blessed.
I danced to smooth, old-school R&B.
Not as old as you like, but songs from the 90s.
I motioned for your great niece to join me.
We danced together holding hands.
We made up words to some of the songs.
Laughter rang throughout the house.
I pranced around doing housework.
My to-do-list was almost complete,
When thoughts of you flooded my mind.
Songs reminded me of our childhood.
A million good thoughts made me smile.
We had epic fights tearing up the house.
We always came together to fix what was broken.
I thought of how we settled our differences.
The older we got some things no longer mattered.
Age differences nor personalities were issues.
Our relationship changed from sisters to friends.
Because of pure and genuine love for each other,
Our Sisterly Bond remains indestructible.
Reminiscing began to ruin my good day.

For most of the day while folding laundry,
The dark cloud over my head was gone.
My every thought was not of you.
I was enjoying a "normal day" of being happy.
I began to feel guilty for leaving you.
I felt guilty for not thinking of you.
Tears flowed because I felt so helpless.
I screamed, I prayed, and I yelled even more.
You are my Big Sis!
You are supposed to be a phone call away!
You are supposed to be helping me through this crisis!
What am I supposed to do without you right now?
I miss you and I miss our talks.
Sometimes, we talked about important stuff.
Other times, we called each other for advice.
A lot of times, hearing each other's voice was enough.
Right now, I need all of them!
I began to wonder about your current state.
You are confined to a room that is not yours.
Are you comfortable in a strange bed?
Do you have enough blankets to keep you warm?
When was the last time you had pain medicine?
Are your vitals stable or within normal range?
Are you breathing completely on your own?
Are they treating you well and attentive to your needs?
Do you feel alone miles and miles away from us?
As I pray for you every day and every night.
I send hugs and kisses through the airways.
I have peace and take comfort in knowing,
You are subconsciously catching each of them.

Love,
Your Lil Sis ❤

Ignite

The steamy room exposes us.
    We silently sit in the aftermath
Of "what have we done,"
As emotions undoubtedly ignite confusion.

Chocolate Covered Excuses

With passion overflowing,
    Chocolate melted perfectly
From the heat of our love.

Gooey streams of deceit and lies
Dipped in the sweetest chocolate
Confused me into believing in you.

The darkness of your many layers
Surprisingly stained my teeth
To unreachable places in my mouth.

The richness of your excuses
Began to pain my mouthwatering tongue
Causing unbearable amounts of agony.

Your delicious words of deception
Tasted delightful with disappointment
Needing no cream or sugar.

The sinfully, tasty bars of truth
Housed securely with someone else
Liquefied my desire to unwillingly leave.

In the end, Chocolate Covered Excuses
Caused more grief than it was worth
Aching my teeth like never before.

Mistakes

Unknown to me as we dated,
    You watched me over the years.
Not from eyes of loving admiration,
But eyes of criticism and imperfection.
Your day in court with witnesses
Has always been your end goal.
Shifting all the blame to me,
You carefully mounted your evidence.
In the rolodex of your mind,
You kept all of my indiscretions.
The ones I had forgotten I made
Were highlighted in yellow.
The irony of my favorite color
Used on my most embarrassing mistakes.
I applauded your tenacity though.
Your note keeping skills were studious.
Well prepared for the attendees in court,
Your opening statement was strong.
Realizing all is not fair in breakups and court,
I raised my right hand repeating the oath.
Opened folders on your prosecution bench,
Destroyed the apologies I humbly gave you.
Sticky notes accompanied mistakes
Made before I ever knew you.
Blown away by the surprising discovery,
I objected to the relevance of my previous life.
Embarrassed by my secrets on display,

The shame on my face misled the jury.
Glancing at your table leaving the witness stand,
More incriminating evidence was barely legible.
These mistakes were written in pencil.
Fresh eraser crumbs burned holes in my mind.
Not sure why the evidence was not brought up.
The neglected information strengthened by defense.
With no intentions of destroying you,
I only wanted to clear my name from the circus.
During my cross examination of you on the stand,
I refused to address you directly and refocused.
One question, Your Honor, and I will rest my case.
Out of all the evidence presented by him today,
Where are my mistakes involving him?
As pressure displayed your ignorance,
I seized victory through your sweat and silence.
All I could hear as I exited the heavy wooden doors,
"Charges have been dropped against the defendant."
With a clean slate and Double Jeopardy on my side,
I left with my mistakes sealed by the court.

Poison in My Belly

Overflowing with a slow, steady desire.
The poison in my belly began to rise.
The toxins craved naughtiness from me.
Causing a constant internal struggle within,
The poison in my belly tried to overtake my senses.
Forcing me to bite or sting to refuel his desires.
I never willingly participated in his feeding sessions.
The beach seemed to be its only temporary antidote.
I wandered aimlessly through the sand some nights.
The ocean's waves were betraying me as they raged.
The full moon aggravated the craving more.
The naughty urges weighted so heavily on me,
The brawl strengthened to a level I've never seen.
As I fought against my unwanted assignment.
One morsel of evilness would end the suffering.
My words became difficult and jumbled.
My skin began to dampen and turn pale.
Closing my eyes to gain some control,
Venom oozed from my ears and mouth.
The beach caught my tumbling body.
Hearing it calling my name through my dizziness,
The poison in my belly craved substance.
Rushing by my side to assist after I passed out,
He gently brushed the sand from my face.

Unaware of my blood shot eyes and my unfilled desire,
His kindness and concern did not deserve my deceit.
I found the perfect victim as it was too late for him.
Closing my eyes after I found the perfect spot to bit him,
The poison in my belly selflessly won once again.

Love Songs in the Rain

The freedom in which I felt as a child,
When Love Songs played in the Rain,
Can be described as enchanting.
I had no clue what the lyrics meant.
It just felt good between my toes.
Thundering and lightning never stopped me
From sitting on the front porch in a storm.
Excitement wrapped around like a blanket,
As Love Songs engaged the Rain.
Flashes across the sky made me giddy.
Rain pounded hard against the pavement
As Love Songs in the Rain grew louder.
The notes I sang blew through tree branches,
Holding my innocence in its strength.
Love Songs in the Rain.

The uncertainty in which I feel as a woman,
When Love Songs come on in the Rain,
Can be described as frightening.
I know the meaning of those Love Songs now,
As the reminders stab the history of the Rain.
I am fearful of another raging storm.
My heart cannot take another downpour.
The sweet Love Songs I sang as a child
Remain restrained in the Rain like a plague.
I hide under the umbrella of disappointments.
Love Songs in the Rain has no destination now.
Drifting unhappily down the middle of the street,

Without a heart to penetrate its floating pain.
Damage is left to be sorted out in the aftermath.
Love Songs in the Rain.

Obligations and Situations

I am not sure when these feelings started.
Loving you completely surprised me.
Working side by side together for years,
We interacted as colleagues and friends.
Projects displayed our creative teamwork
As our chemistry was felt by the both of us.
You became braver than I ever was
Planting ideas of us being together.
Excitement reached untouched levels.
I was shocked by the new development.
I tried to hide the growing feelings for you.
Often, I wondered if you sensed my secret,
While I constantly spoke contrasting words.
Responding to your advances was unacceptable.
There was no way to make our obsession work.
We had other commitments after 6:00pm.
Our families' lives were complicated.
Obligations and situations!
Obligations and situations!
Obligations and situations!
Still, I wished I could have you.
The desire to see you strengthened.
Unable to find words to express my thoughts,
I hung out a little longer than I should have
Hoping to bump into you.
My heart began to yearn for more.
More than coffee and conversations.
More than lunch breaks and secret meetings.
The water cooler talks were no longer enough.

The restaurants were of no desire anymore.
I wished we could walk freely in our attraction.
No hidden phone calls or confidential emails.
Slow walks in the park holding hands.
Late night rendezvous exploring our love.
I had fallen for you, and I was lost in those feelings.
Lost in the waves of emotions I could not escape.
Loving someone I wish I could have
Tortured my soul as the days went by.
Confused on how to proceed if I should.
Thoughts of my family began to trump everything.
My wants and needs reluctantly stayed at the office
Awaiting my return on the next day to be entertained.
Obligations and situations!
Obligations and situations!
Obligations and situations!

Does Love?

Does love come with trust, honesty, and loyalty anymore?

Can You?

Can you look beyond my pretty face
    And see a blossoming future with me?
Can you?

Can you look beyond the brownness in my eyes
And see a woman who will love you through your scars?
Can you?

Can you look beyond the fullness of my lips
And see someone who will speak life into you?
Can you?

Can you look beyond the curves in my hips
And see my mind is more attractive?
Can you?

Can you look beyond my piercing and tattoos
And see a beautifully expressed canvas?
Can you?

Can you look beyond my imperfections
And see my true beauty is my soul?
Can you?

Give Back... You Didn't

Give back...
　Give back my uniqueness, my distinctiveness, my energy.
Give back my confidence, my self-esteem, my vibe.
Give back my smile, my happiness, my love for people.
You didn't appreciate those things about me anyways.
You didn't...

Give back...
Give back my understanding, my sympathy, my empathy.
Give back my trust, my loyalty, my honesty.
Give back my thoughts, my time, my faithfulness.
You didn't value those things about me anyways.
You didn't...

Give back...
Give back my tears, my mind, my love.
Give back my prayers, my hopes, my dreams.
Give back my independence, my peace of mind, my hopefulness.
You didn't acknowledge those things about me anyways.
You didn't...

Give back...
Give back my innocence, my hope in love, my ways of doing things.
Give back my missed Girls Nights, my ruined dinners, our ruined dates.
Give back my good deeds, my unspoken words, my hope for tomorrow.
You didn't trust those things about me anyways.
You didn't...

Give back…
Give back our family, our vacations, our hand holding.
Give back our inside jokes, our working together, our completed projects.
Give back your favorite snack, my favorite snack, our favorite snack.
You didn't treasure those things about me anyways.
You didn't...

Give back…
Give back your clean laundry, my completed chores, my devotion.
Give back cooked dinners, prepared breakfasts, packed lunches.
Give back my independence, my self-evaluation, my self-esteem.
You didn't cherish those things about me anyways.
You didn't...

Give back…
Give back our love, our pillow talks, my engagement ring.
Give back our wedding date, our wedding plans, my wedding dress.
Give back my shame of no wedding, my pride, my embarrassment.
You didn't respect those things about me anyways.
You didn't...

Give it back because you just didn't...
You... JUST...Didn't!

Loving You from Over Here

Years ago, I would have bet anything
On you being in my life forever
As my lover and not just my friend.
Loving you from over here
Does not feel good or feel the same.
I do not want this watered-down relationship!
I want you like I had you when I had you.
Other relationships pale in comparison,
Lacking our level of mad, crazy intensity.
Our wasted passion follows and taunts me.
I cannot devour or handle others like I did you.
Filling the void from needing you in my life,
I settled for your friendship I do not want!
Loving you from over here
Forced me to create a new norm.
Mentally and physically exhausted
Because I still feel you everywhere.
My new normal life is filled with cravings
For the uniqueness and specialness of you.
You always made my problems go away.
Never allowing them to penetrate our time.
You squeezed the very breath out of their bodies.
You provided a protected space of peace.
I became so comfortable around you.
Comfortable enough to shed layers of myself.
I discovered things about me through your love.
We built a tranquility of unspoken truths.
Your house and you became my sanctuaries.
You were perfect for me and my life.

Our love was pure excellence at its finest.
You are the most amazing person I know
With a winning personality and a sense of humor.
Loving you from over here
Forces me to walk down memory lane.
Some nights our bodies entwined.
Some nights our love did all the talking.
In your arms from your bedroom window,
The new morning sky made me smile.
The grass was greener. The air was crisper.
The birds chirped louder. The wind blew more gentle.
Loving you from over here,
Concepts lack the same meaning and value.
Freedom from you becomes my new imprisonment.
Dating is oppressed by thoughts of you.
The sun still rises over the horizon at your house.
The view is not as bright from my side of town.
I had to confront the differences through my pain
Without the security of your arms around me.
Loving you from over here,
Was never meant to be experienced
Alone in front of my window with you over there.

Changes

Seasons always change

Feelings frequently change

Love evidently changes

You surprisingly changed

I reluctantly changed

Life unwillingly changed

Stuck Between Two Loves

I lost everything stuck between Two Loves one day.
   It started harmless, carefree, and uncomplicated.
The void in my life did not have an issue with my Two Loves.
Each of them served a purpose in filling the black hole's craving.
One was structured, which formed my disciplined side.
The other was creative, which sparked my artistic side.
I became a better person because of my Two Loves.
Stuck equally between Two Loves required delicate handling.
Neglecting here to go play and be satisfied over there.
Hiding and ducking over there when I should be here.
Catering to my Two Loves caused me to become selfish.
I loved my Two Loves more than I hated my actions.
The necessary lies for me to continue to play strengthened.
Stuck between Two Loves became my new obsession.
One Love was too complicated holding his position the longest.
Other Love was easy going feeling like we had a lifetime together.
I was annoyed by the constant check-ins with One Love.
My extra time was the only requirement by my Other Love.
One Love was judgmental injuring me with his words.
Other Love listened intently telling me I had a way with words.
One Love never knew the real me after all those years.
Other Love understood everything about me.
Stuck between Two Loves grew more intensely complicated.
I skillfully played faithful girlfriend and naughty girlfriend,
Splitting my time equally between Two Loves.
Too deep in my commitments to my Loves to stop the circus.
The merry-go-round of honesty had no effect on me.

Floating pieces of me attached itself to what felt like home.
My ego and my void needed my Loves to survive.
Understanding and perception fought constantly for my attention.
Distorting comprehension of basic facts rested in a wasteland.
Love and being in love fought constantly for my heart.
Unfair daggers landed on bystanders waiting for my Two Loves.
Independence and constraint fought for my state of mind.
The battle flag hung at half mass ashamed of my foolishness.
Declaration of War and blissfulness brawled for my approval.
Compromising cloud nine's strength was a growing concern.
Decisions needing to be made were muddled with feelings.
One Love challenged his position in my life with a ring.
Other Love simply asked me to choose him, and only him.
Choosing neither of my Two Loves, I selfishly chose me.
The security of One Love and Other Love were too vital.
The arrangement was never scripted parts meant to last forever.
The stage play ended with my unwillingness to choose.
My Love exited left because I did not choose him.
Other Love exited right since I refused to decide.
Left with my void, my selfishness, and my shame,
My heart gets stick from the memories of the show titled,
"Stuck Between Two Loves."

Grandma

Grandma always told us to believe half of what we see and none of what we hear. Life has taught me Grandma might have been on to something.

Chapter III:
Socially Conscious

Mask

With your mask on or your mask off, you will have to deal with the consequences of your many faces publicly and privately.

Hands Up

Privilege rides in the car with you.
    Law and Order seep through your window,
Mirroring the hatred in your heart.
Exercising your oath to serve,
You scream at me, "Hands Up,"
My hands have been up,
Fighting the injustice against my people.
My closed fist intimidates you.
My skin color annoys you.
So much so, my basic rights are ignored.
You choke me, shoot me, and beat me
With or without resistance.
Silent or violent protests are the same.
Another life lost at your hands.
You receive a Badge of Honor for your services,
From the one-sided account of the body cam.
My people attempt to restore my tarnished reputation,
A celebration of life and a yearly day of remembrance.
No winners in this vicious cycle of blue,
With a Justice System protecting only you.

Generational Thinking

Generational thinking has me torn up inside,
    As Momma's and Auntie's "Golden Rules"
Ring ever so loud.
"You hustle Girl, and you hustle hard."
"Don't let your right hand know what you left hand is doing."
"Life is more rewarding when you don't depend on a man."
Generational thinking has me torn up inside!
Witnessing my family falling apart through lies.
Arguments over honesty, mistrust, and lack of loyalty.
Protecting oneself in a marriage of two.
Sighing and shaking my head…
My kids will never witness dysfunction like that!
Generational thinking has me torn up inside.
Surely, there is an achievable middle ground,
    Between the way I was raised and the way I want to be.
I want my man to hold my left hand before God,
Leading me into untrodden territory with his right.
As I hustle, together we hustle harder.
Together, securing our future and our bag.
Hold up Sis! Don't hold him too closely though.
"'Cause remember you don't need a man."
Generational thinking has me torn up inside!
Dealing with someone not worthy of being in my life.
Happiness or loyalty, which will it be?
It can only be one… just one,
    According to Momma's and Auntie's philosophies.

Generational thinking has me torn up inside!
Sitting by this window with thoughts so heavy,
I fight back the tears I now hold inside.
My corrections of generation thinking
Created a new dysfunction.
Watching things manifest in my child's life
Directly related from the things I taught him.
Forcing him to choose between his own future
Or promises he should never have made.
But I, it was me, who taught him
To be honest, be trustworthy, and be loyal.
The apple didn't fall from the tree,
This generational thinking started with me!

The House on Main Street

Red door and black shutters adjoined.
Sweet Peas and Marigolds aligned.
Flowerpots carefully arranged.
2.5-inch grass blades manicured.
The porch perfectly decorated.
Beautiful curtains closed.
Newest foreign cars parked.
Diluted mirage falsified.
The House on Main Street.

Abuse successfully concealed.
Groceries regularly delivered.
Friendly waves unreturned.
Eye contact avoided.
Off-season clothing worn.
Overlarge sunglasses sported.
Black and blue bruises hidden.
Intense depression noticed.
The House on Main Street.

Children perfectly dressed.
Playdates declined.
Good grades achieved.
School activities evaded.
Befriending classmates shunned.
Self-esteem recognizably depleted.
Safe welfare not sensed.
Sadness from their eyes eluded.
The House on Main Street.

Piercing screams stifled.
Muffled cries smothered.
Alarming noises oppressed.
Family nor friends visited.
Mail and newspapers stacked.
Comings and goings not noticed.
Broken furniture discarded.
Bedroom windows smashed.
The House on Main Street.

Crime scene taped.
Evidence safely preserved.
Photographs and notes extracted.
Police and investigators probed.
Neighbors in crowds gathered.
Rumors rapidly circulated.
Black body bags removed.
Domestic Violence established.
The House on Main Street.

War Cry

The War Cry from a black mother
Can be heard late in the midnight hour.
It sounds like a broken drum,
Penetrating your heart and your soul.
I began to mourn of a life not known.
In the comfort of my bedroom,
I sympathize with a black mother's suffering.
Across country, a son is being buried
From an untimely and senseless death.
Across town, a daughter desperately looks for drugs
In the streets that do care or love her.
Our black women are being killed,
With doors securely locked
In their very own homes without regrets.
My black son came home tonight
And I still can't relax enough to breathe.
There may not be a knee on his throat,
But my windpipe is crushed from unshed tears.
The War Cry from a black mother
Takes my ability away to control myself.
The dam finally breaks pushing my emotions
Into an unsafe and dangerous place.
I grieve for the broken pieces of my community
Existing far too long and growing stronger.
I pray my optimism remains at its best,
While Systematic Racism is at its worst.
Basic needs to survive in our community,
Become desired items or unfulfilled wishes.
Our lives are literally put on the line every day.

Without just cause, we are shot
In our backs, our heads, or our chests.
No place seems safe for our black men to escape.
Punishable crimes take our boys away for years,
While other boys receive slaps on the wrists.
We walked, sweated, and bled for voting rights.
Attempts with bogus lies try to strip them from us.
Enough never seems to be enough
When 2021 is a replicate of 1600.
Things are far from "separate but equal,"
As I open my eyes and coexist in this world.
Our housing, our jobs, and our school systems
Are vastly different setting us up for failure.
A black mother's War Cry simply wants more.
More time with her deceased son or daughter.
More space in a house she can barely afford.
More opportunities to excel in her career.
Books and caring teachers in her children's classrooms.
The War Cry from a black mother,
Simply wants change in her world
So, she can live in harmony and peace.

Where, When What Happened?

Darkness was all around the room
　　As grief took over her mind.
Her cell phone laid halfway in her hand.
The other half grazed the floor.
The blinds remained opened.
Streetlights shined brightly in the house.
Her incomplete dinner was ruined.
Smoke filled the house as the alarm sounded.
Lost hours of time could not be rewound.
An illogical explanation wandered in the streets.
The same streets holding innocent blood
Like decades from the past.
Another mother has to deal with blue corruption.
Unsolved police shootings swept under the rug.
One phone call changed her world as she knew it.
No mention of a police shooting on the 6:00 news.
Maybe Channel 5 was gathering all the facts.
Previous news stories could not soften the blow!
Did they say he was shot and identify his body?
He was where, when what happened?
Countless tears rolled down her cheeks.
She could not open her eyes nor move her legs.
The confusion must be a nightmare.
Her son planned a normal day.
Classes in the morning.
Part-time job in the evening.
Only a block, 200 feet, away from campus.
Willing to bet her son was nothing but polite.
She was sure he used yes ma'am and no sir.

Her son never started or engaged in trouble.
Confrontation was not his motive or agenda.
His greatness was wrapped in brown skin.
Threats became present even in non-hostile situations.
Their morning talk was fresh in her mind.
He was nervous about his last couple of finals.
Graduation was next week.
Ready to be achieved and celebrated.
White, blue, and red lights rolled down her street.
The same lights meant for Graduation Day.
No congratulations or balloons were attached.
Freedom was not represented in the land of the free
As her son senselessly lost his life that day.

Comparisons and Confusion

Way too much woman for comparison with a twig.
Promises to break standards if you place me amid.
Being a Real One requires my man's mind to config.
Seeing only my loyalty and honesty are off the grid.

Killing our black boys have become their new drug.
Injustice I pray away as my heartstrings tug.
Unjustified reasoning, I see even when my mind unplugs.
Discrimination is why I greet and leave you with hugs.

Your song lyrics have messages that underline.
The impoverished state we live in, they define.
Our empowerment lies tucked away in our rhymes.
Power in numbers as we urge our people to combine.

Profiting and taking advantage of our compassion,
We need to bankrupt these fools by creating our own fashion.
Tearing our families apart with names on their dockets.
In their systems is where they gain the most profits.

A Good Friend But a Bad Girl

Sitting behind the metal bars in jail,
    I thought of all the fun I had the weekend.
I was a Good Friend but a Bad Girl.
The people I encountered last night had morals,
Protecting the safety of the old, quaint establishment.
The dancing lights, fruity drinks, and handsome entertainment
Caused my hands to explore the attractions on stage.
Momma told me to keep my hands to myself,
While living in the house with five other people.
That teaching went out the window last night,
Landing me on such an uncomfortable bench.
The jailor haltered my raging thoughts,
Reminding me of my one phone call.
Completely ignoring the time zone differences,
I was a Bad Girl but a Good Friend at 3:00am in the morning.
I called my one Good Friend I knew would rescue me,
Since we landed ourselves in similar positions together before.
While I promised I would not be a Bad Girl without her,
My greeting along with the collect call made her nervous.
I told her where the "get of jail money" was stashed
With my most innocent version of my night's dealing.
Trying not to incriminate myself over the phone,
I expected our Love Language of Trouble to fill in the blanks.
Clicks and a silenced line alerted my time ran out.
As I was hastily escorted back to my holding cell,
I prayed my Good Friend deciphered the cryptic message.
Hours later, my Good Friend walked through the door.
Smiling and waiting to hear the juicy details of my weekend,
As she knew I was a Good Friend but a Bad Girl.

I Didn't Want to Die That Day

I was on display in town before master's dinner.
The crowd was enthusiastic and excited for the show.
Their promptness showed their true characters.
Not the kind found in the pages of the Bible.
Familiar scriptures were read to support their foolishness.
Their encouraging words didn't mean the same to me.
Misconstrued interpretations became their bases.
Handing out beatings in hopes of keeping us all in line.
I didn't want to die that day!
Chants for injustice were heard over my silent cries.
My family was forced to bear witness to the punishment.
Unmanageable tears fell on an unwelcoming ground.
My wife and children watching the events pained me,
More than the brutality already received and yet to come.
Pleading my case until the last possible second,
My wife refused to break her grip on me.
Her tug-of-war could have been our last time together.
I didn't want to die that day!
My shirt was barely hanging on my beaten body.
The punishment started from the plantation.
Master dragged me faster than I could walk.
My shoes were unrecognizable exposing my swollen feet.
Most of my toenails were left on the bloody trail.
My pants were ripped from top to bottom
My waistband didn't remain intact.
I was soiled from my own sweat and blood.
I didn't want to die that day!
My family's current death threats weakened me.
Mental games began to break my spirit,

Physically and emotionally battering me.
Couldn't show my strength though.
I let them put shackles on my hands and feet.
I let them push me roughly to the ground.
I let them spit and urinate on me without a fight.
My family and my life were literally at stake.
I didn't want to die that day!
I vividly remembered the first lash.
The 35th lash didn't quite feel like the first one.
The 63rd one paled in comparison too.
The 91st lash did not convince me either.
Not even the 100th lash felt like the first one.
Each lash damaged me in its own unique way.
They degraded me and ripped me of my pride.
Taunting words from the crowd destroyed my ego.
I didn't want to die that day!
Master left me on the carved wood for hours.
My shredded skin and loosen teeth laid upon it,
Barely giving room for my pounding head to rest.
Blood, so much blood, poured from my body.
The scarlet warmth ran down the streets in town.
The faster the flow, the more enticed they became.
There are no words left in my exhausted body.
Nothing can verbalize the pain I felt anyways.
I didn't want to die that day!
No credit was given because they didn't kill me.
They stripped me of what made me a man.
Petrified to look my wife in the eyes.
Afraid my kids wouldn't look up to me.
Other slaves might not respect me anymore.
Pondering if master would be satisfied after the beating,
Whispers of bartering began between a mule and me.
The wounded animal was fortunately victorious.
I didn't want to die that day!

FREE

How FREE are we if we are riding on the backs of generations enslaved before us, to be treated as second best today?

Chapter IV:

Inspired by God

Sweet Life

How sweet is life on the other side of revamped plans, which previously yield "no's"?!

What Are You Trying to Tell Me?

Ringing phones are heard throughout the office.
    Fedex and UPS deliver numerous, unexpected packages.
Short on employees causes pure chaos on deadlines.
A vision of complete calmness stops me in my tracks.
What are you trying to tell me?

Traffic is unusually crazy and extremely busy.
My enjoyable music is interrupted to report a crime.
There are no dinner ideas floating in my mind.
A vision of peace and serenity totally surrounds me.
What are you trying to tell me?

Winding down for the night from pure exhaustion,
A Prayer of Thanksgiving is quick and sufficient.
My priorities are flipping through the TV and not praying to God.
A vision of elevation shows my answered prayers.
What are you trying to tell me?

Disobedience and undisciplined areas exist in my life.
My life is overflowing with blessings I did not ask.
Undeserved grace and mercy are extended to me daily.
A vision of living water flows steadily on my feet.
What are you trying to tell me?

Dear God

Is "Thank You" enough to express my most sincerest gratitude?

I Found Her

I found her broken, lost, and incomplete.
She cried the same familiar tears night after night.
Barely having money left after rent, daycare, and food,
She had no choice but to work one dead in job after another.

She often wondered why I was punishing her,
Discouraged because life dealt her a tough hand.
Making a deal with me to see if I was real,
She poured out her heart in pure desperation.

She went to church often with her son in tow.
I still found her given up on life and herself.
As the same familiar tears flowed from her eyes,
I found my daughter lost in a world that is not mine.

Hearing testimonies of others attesting of my goodness,
Skeptically, she began to study my promises in the Bible.
She began to talk with me and started to walk like me.
One day, she could no longer resist my tug on her heart.

She ran to the alter begging, "What must I do to be saved?"
I comforted her by gently grabbing my daughter's hand.
Wiping away those same familiar tears in my embrace,
I found her on the day when she was ready to find me.

Garden of Despair

Hidden in the Garden of Despair,
The weeds were tall enough to hide me.
I found comfort there,
In the cool, moist dirt under the ground.
The thickened soil helped me,
As it hid my uncontainable tears.
My heart hardened like the bug's shell,
Whose personal space I invaded.
Because of my own hopelessness,
The Garden of Despair is all I saw.
God's promises were mucked
By my own dirty misunderstandings.
The ground toughened with each wiggle,
Causing my mess to get deeper,
As I tossed dirt on my own back.
The man-made Garden of Despair
Was built to bring life in the world.
My dim present destroyed its purpose.
The sun slipped behind the moon
Fertilizing my misguided emotions.
The lack of oxygen underground
Suffocated the last ray of hope.
Succumbing to the living condition,
I caused permanent stains on my blessings.
I honestly lost track of the day and time,
As the Crabgrass held my loneliness.
Never requiring payment for its services,
The Garden of Despair became dangerous.
The Day Lilies and Tulips I once loved,

Could not take root and grow down here.
Remaining completely silent with no prayers,
I chose to remain in the Garden of Despair
Not yielding any profitable or sustainable fruit.
The sprouting Dandelions gave me hope,
As the brightness of the weeds shook the ground.
Ripping the disharmony in the Garden of Despair,
I winced from the penetration of Tea Weed's thorns.
I felt something different coursing through me.
A breath of forgiveness rested in my lungs,
As God's arms held me closely to his heart.
He found me broken and incomplete,
Yearning for his love in the Garden of Despair.

Pride

Boastfulness validated who I created myself to be.
Loneliness was the only companion sharing my home.
Family and friends disappeared years ago.
My Pride was not welcomed or handled by the weak.
Often, my bed had mates with alternative motives.
Their greed escorted them out before I slept.
A replacement will warm the same spot soon.
My Pride only needed feeding for a couple of hours.
I celebrated my accomplishments with luxurious gifts.
Expensive breadcrumbs laced the bottom of my shoes.
No one was worthy enough to drink my champagne.
My Pride reminded me of my earned elevation of privilege.
Tossing demands and undervaluing others were my specialties.
No time to tell God thank you for all He has done.
Those seconds were used to build my empire even higher.
My Pride drove me to thank myself and conquer more.
The dollar signs sealed the constant pain in my chest.
Stress supplied the commas in my bank accounts.
A bed of affliction was slowly developing as my reward.
My Pride only cared about my name on the building.
Poor judgement and my career led me to destruction.
As labor breathing resounded through my extremities,
My Pride unwillingly ushered my feeble body on the ride.
The bright lights and the siren disclosed my destination.
Released with no one by my side, life did not feel the same.
Suddenly, I longed for familiar faces I once pushed away.
My fancy cars and designer clothes offered no comfort.
Longing for family and old friends opened new wounds.

The new prescription drugs did not ease the pain.
My Pride had little to say or even cared about my situation.
Thinking I am weak and not worthy of his time,
My Pride departed as humbling itself was not an option.
He rather let "the rocks cry out" for him. (Luke 19:40, KJV)
On bended knees, I chose a different path than my Pride.
Restoring relationships, especially with God, was my new focus.
One day at a time, my new life looked better without my Pride.

Favor

Not Accidental
 Nor Coincidental,
  God's Undeserving Favor
  Is Intentional!

Recommitted

Ongoing health issues had me in a fog.
My passion and my drive were gone.
I no longer felt like myself.
I no longer looked like myself.
I accepted negative thoughts in my life
Created by fear of the unknown.
I robbed myself of life's joy.
My mind was all over the place.
I showed up from time to time
Only presenting the good side of me.
The tormented side of me was at home
Sorting through torturing thoughts.
Due to the pain in my body,
My supportive nature was gone.
Family or friends no longer saw my smile.
The sun was not shining through me anymore,
Only darkness lived within and around me.
I was completely depleted from the battle.
My attention was solely on the disease.
I entered a phase of not living
Existing from one chemo pill to the next.
Fridays felt like Tuesdays.
Tuesdays felt like Fridays.
My pen dried up with my motivation.
I barely wrote anything
Nor did I have a desire to do so.
My embarrassing thoughts were safe in my head
Or at least I prayed they were.
One dark and lonely night I decided,

I was tired of wobbling in pain.
Remembering the only help I know,
I dusted the cobwebs from my knees.
Praying for total forgiveness,
I began to trust God again for my healing.
My body and my mind needed a touch from him.
Quoting and believing my favorite scriptures,
Slowly, I looked and felt like myself.
My strength came back each day.
I recommitted to loving myself.
I recommitted to writing my poetry.
I recommitted to fulfilling my personal mission,
I was going to do better and be better!
I recommitted!

Blessings

Take the bad with the good until the wind blows God's blessings all over your life again.

About the Author

Katrina A. McCain grew up in a small town named Nashville, NC where 5500 people reside. Having big dreams and bigger goals, Katrina relocated to Greensboro, NC in 2004, where she currently lives. After settling in Greensboro, for a couple of years, Katrina completed her *Bachelor of Science in Accounting* at Guilford College. She currently works as an Accountant at a non-profit agency serving the youth in Guilford County and surrounding areas. As a proud published author of her poetry book titled, "Because She Decided to Love;" Katrina has been featured in Poet Speak Magazine, Influential Women Who Win, and Blessings Magazine. Since the release of her first poetry book, "Because She Decided To Love," she created her own Cross Market Monday Shows in which she highlights other small business owners and entrepreneurs. Katrina created an Author Spotlight as another way to give back by providing reviews on other author's books she has read. As if that was not enough, Katrina also formed a "Relay for Life" team appropriately named, "Team McCain." Each year, she raises money for The American Cancer Society not only to support her own personal battle with cancer, but to also support others the battle against cancer. A dedicated member of her family goes without saying as the Publisher, Author, Poet, Businesswoman, Entrepreneur demonstrates how family comes first in Katrina's life.

Follow Katrina A. McCain

Website: www.poetkatrinamccain.com

Facebook: www.facebook.com/poetkatrinamccain

Instagram: www.instagram.com/poetkatrinamccain

Twitter: www.twitter.com/McCainPoet

YouTube: Poet Katrina McCain

Other Books

by Katrina A McCain

Because She Decided to Love:
Poems of Love & Relationships

Upcoming Projects

Katrina A. McCain is currently working on a Collection of Short Stories. Here is a sneak preview featuring the short story titled, "Fragile Love with Glass Affections."

Fragile Love with Glass Affections

I woke up with hazy, glazed eyes and wondered exactly where I was before the ache in my heart reminded me of the recent events I wanted to forget. The weight of lies and deception rested heavily in the middle of my chest, and I did not want to move or breathe or think or feel. There was no way I had been receiving Fragile Love with Glass Affections for a year now. How can something so beautiful and strong have me torn up inside? A tear followed by more tears escaped my eyes as I squeezed them together tighter in hopes of stopping the steady stream now soaking my pillow. Feeling stupid and used by love, I gave into the raw emotions building inside of me.

After another soul cleansing cry, I glanced at my phone. I had seventy-two missed calls and two hundred and nine unanswered texts from the last five days since I have been running from the world. I knew a couple of them were from my momma since she can sense when something is wrong with her baby. Have I really been drowning in my sorrows behind a Fragile Love with Glass Affections? Too weak mentally to respond to any of the notifications on my phone, I tossed it on the other side of the bed with no interest as to where it landed. The last time I had interest to do anything was five nights ago when I pleaded for a position in her heart and in her life. When did the tables turn where I was cut from the shards of Glass Affections with Fragile Love?

Replaying the events in my mind of what landed me in this bed, I vividly recalled the night I met her. It was a cold January night, and the wind was blowing so strongly it cut through the night sky. I worked sixty-five hours the last two weeks straight and I was

exhausted from everything involving those weeks. The take-out from multiple restaurants all tasted the same. Each night of sleep felt like the night before feeling like I only slept for five minutes. The coffee tasted bland each morning and my work-out routine was neglected so I did not have the necessary energy to pass my front door. I did not know if I wore black suits each day to work or if I chose a variety of other colors. My suitcase was an extension of my body since it I was within two feet of me. My mind was in overdrive as we had two influential clients' projects with the same deadline.

Before she and her Fragile Love with Glass Affections came into my life on a Friday night. I think I dozed off in the shower. I was exhausted from looking at blueprints and all of its revisions. I dreamed the clients rejected the perfect proposals and I had to repeat the last 3 months of work. I glanced at the clock several times once the sun started to rise the next morning. I really needed to work out since I skipped the gym from the demands at work the last two weeks. My bed held me hostage and I succumbed to its demands without a fight. When I finally decided I had enough sleep, the growl from my stomach echoed loudly throughout my condo. How long have I been asleep? The ringing of my phone brought me out of my sleepy trance, and I immediately recognized the number.

Catching up with one of my homeboys from college was always a great time. Since several of us were free, we decided to go to the newly opened Grown and Sexy Lounge in town. All the reviews about the place were raving with lines around the block with people waiting to enter. The night was no exception as we waited 30 minutes to enter the lounge. Immediately, I was impressed by the lounge's atmosphere and all the beautiful people it attracted. The lights were low, the music was dope, and the dance floor was crowded. Wanting to get my round of drinks out the way, I headed to the bar and placed the usual order for the crew. I laughed to myself because we've been friends 20 years

and nobody's drinking preference had changed. As I waited on the Bartender to return with our drinks, I saw the most beautiful creature I have ever seen, and I could not take my eyes off of her. She was on the dance floor with two ladies, who looked to be her sisters, and a group of other beautiful ladies dancing to one of the latest Line Dancing Song. The way she swayed her hips and perked her lips to her moves caught my attention immediately.

As soon as I put our drinks down on our table, I had to meet her. I sipped on my crisp, cold beer and I watched how the captivating lady commanded the room with her mannerism. She was absolutely beautiful the way she carried herself. She had on a tight black dress showing the right amount of thighs, which got me excited. The jacket she wore over the dress told me she was a classy lady, and a night club would not change how she presented herself to the world. Those 3-inch heels she wore sealed the deal for me. She looked to be 5'5" with the prettiest light brown skin.

The club was dark and smoky from the effects the DJ used to make his music seem a little more appealing. The facade did not dull the radiance coming from her smile. Thinking I am just as extraordinary as she is, I made my move before she left with her girls. I quickly walked to her side of the club with no pickup line or pre-played conversation in mind. She did not deserve any line I used on another lady or any pickup line I ever thought of before. Feet away from her now, I smiled at her as she turned in my direction and she smiled back. I extended my hand, introduced myself, and said "It is nice to meet you." She grabbed my hand and seductively told me her name. I found myself smiling like a chess cat as I talked to her for the rest of the night. My intentions were to lead her to the dance floor after getting her attention to have her closer to me. The vibe between us was so strong, we exchanged numbers to keep in touch. Somehow, I missed

the yellow neon sign flashing, "Warning: She is capable of Fragile Love with Glass Affections."

Months turned into a year as I began to know her deeper than any other love interest in my life. When things are going great for me in my personal life, my past or current lies always have a way of catching up to me. All of my troubles began one night after going on a date with her. Interrupting the smooth R&B music playing throughout the sound system in my car, the dashboard screen displayed a familiar phone number. I knew I would have to face the skeletons in my closet after ending the call from a button on the steering wheel. Trying to remain cool, I did not acknowledge the phone call in hopes she would not say anything. Wrong! Her questions were so direct, I could not think of a lie or anything to cover or explain my after-hours phone call. I hesitantly answered her questions with spacing in between my words to avoid trapping myself. She told me to stop talking before she lost respect for me, and I instantly knew our relationship had changed.

The car ride home was miserable and for the first time I could not read the vibes from my lady. The radio echoed louder inside the car and the streetlights flashed brighter outside the car. It was as if they knew I was busted. I thought the secret of my other lover would go to the grave with me since she never pressed me about who I was with or where I was going ever. Splitting my time between two beautiful ladies did not mean I gave Fragile Love with Glass Affections to either of them. I gave both ladies the best of me, within reasonable limits, when I was with them. Now I stand at a crossroad I created, powerless and with no control.

Before the car came to a complete stop, she jumped out and slammed the door. I did not like seeing anyone hurting, especially me, behind my actions. I raced to her side of the car hoping to grasp her before

she reached her doorsteps. I have been in the position countless times when a lady screamed the very same words to me, "I do not want to ever see you again," but those words never stung like that before. Now
with the truth of who I was and what I have been up to standing between us like an uninvited guest, I was paralyzed as to what to say. Tears choked her words as she snatched from my embrace. I followed her up the steps before I decided to let things settle down for the night while she was slamming the door in my face.

Days seemed like eternities before she took my phone call. She calmly said we needed to talk and asked if I could come over. I suggested we go to her favorite restaurant having dinner and some wine to lessen the tension the conversation was surely to bring. She disagreed and told me she thought privacy would be best. I played every possible scenario in my mind as to how the night would end. Would I end up with just one of my ladies in my life or would I end up in bed wrapped around her with all forgotten and forgiven? Only time would tell as I hoped cupid was on my side.

Before I walked out the door to her house, I planned the perfect route to pick up her favorite wine, her favorite chocolate, a little "I'm sorry" gift, and arrive on time. I was nervous feeling like I was walking into a lion's den instead of one of my ladies' houses. I took deep breaths to calm my nerves and I reminded myself she loved me and was crazy about me as I was about her. I listened to my go-to-playlist in the car, and I felt better about the conversation I was going to have. I was not ready to leave my other lady, but I was willing to do whatever it took to keep her in my life. She might not have demanded anything if the dashboard in my car had not betrayed me. Since I was busted, I was willing to be completely honest during our previous conversations about my past life and the playthings I had in it.

She was extremely nervous, just like I was again, when I walked through the front door. She had soft music playing and I could smell her favorite candle lingering in the air. She prepared dinner after I offered a hundred times to stop for takeout. She was so amazing and was still willing to prepare dinner after our breakup. We talked, made promises, set new ground rules, enjoyed a warm bath, I rubbed her feet, and we brought in the new day celebrating our relationship. Our breakup would soon be a thing of our past and so was my other relationship if I wanted to keep "our new rules." Should I have seen the writing on the wall to prevent me from laying in the bed in a cabin tucked away in the woods today reminiscing over Fragile Love with Glass Affections?

As she slept so peacefully, my mind ran to the other side of town where my other lady was. I could not deny the physical connection I had with her and it was like no physical connection I ever had with anyone. Our souls were attracted to each other with a magnetic force neither of us could explain. I never figured out if what we had was real or if our physical connection was Fragile Love with Glass Affections. We enjoyed the ride of our mutual understanding of not defining us with titles or labels and not asking questions when were not together. The relationship worked perfectly for the busy lifestyle I lived. Now approaching thirty-five, it was probably time for me to settle down with one lady. I thought I made progress when I settled down with just two.

The next morning, we skipped our usual Saturday morning walk/run in the park we often did when we both had time. The reconnection last night felt so great and new beginnings were ahead of us. I knew what my heart and mind felt, but I could not let go of the different vibe from her. She seemed closed off and guarded yet she smiled the same. Her eyes were not as warming and caring as they usually were. I chalked it up to the hurt caused by my actions and our new

arrangement would take time. Every time I caught a glimpse of her eyes, the sickening feeling grew deeper in the pit of my stomach. There was no need to worry about all the minor details right now as long as we were on a good path to recovery. I asked her if we were good throughout the morning, and she assured me we were fine.

Time went by and all seemed forgiven by her. We fell into a new groove which was better than before. I was proud to say I was truly a one lady's man and I no longer offered Fragile Love with Glass Affections. One night after dancing the night away with my lady, I told her I loved her. I saw a promising future between us. What I did not tell her was I planned the perfect proposal on her upcoming birthday. As we overlook the balcony somewhere exotic, I would get on my knee and ask her to marry me. I could not decide between three of the rings I picked so I reached out to her best friend for help. Getting her dad's permission for his daughter's hand in marriage was the last thing to make the perfect birthday for her and me. Things were amazing at work and at home and I could not be happier. I have never experienced that type of stability in my personal life and I have to admit, it felt good. Who was that new version of me and could I trust the version of me even if I did not recognize me without the Fragile Love With Glass Affections?

A couple of days before her birthday, I opened the front door of her place. Laughter and music greeted me as I turned the knob. I could have gone to my place and showered before coming over if I knew she was entertaining. I peeked my head in the dining room and spoke to my lady and her friends. After I put my gym bag and jacket away, I decided to get a beer and find something on TV before I showered. Walking down the hallway, I noticed all the laughter stopped and the mood in the house shifted. Obviously, they were whispering about the latest gossip one of them heard. As I turned to head back to her room not to invade their privacy, her best friend's voice rose a little higher

and more aggressively than I think she meant for it. I heard her tell my lady, "Imagine how I felt helping him pick out a ring for you when I know your secret." My legs wanted to continue moving in the
opposite direction or maybe out the front door, but I was glued to the floor. I remembered thinking I should not walk in the dining room to interrupt their conversation to keep my perfect relationship intact. It was hard to un-hear the whispers carrying secrets she was hiding from me.

She walked in her bedroom to ask if she could bring me anything and to tell me her girls would be leaving soon. I told her do not send her girls away and I was going home for the evening. Instantly knowing I heard their conversation, she excused herself to dismiss her friends. I heard whispers amongst them again and the house went quiet. What had she been up to, and would I be able to forgive her? My heart shattered at the thought of another Fragile Love with Glass Affections moment. The only problem was I was the one getting cut. She started the conversation by saying she was not looking for what we developed when we met. I aggressively told her to get to the point because I was getting agitated by her stalling. Tears welled up in her eyes as she carefully explained her story of deception.

Fragile Love with Glass Affections did not supposed to happen to me. Being a man with the best features and the perfect height, I never had problems attracting ladies or indecent propositions. Depending on the way the wind blew; I indulged in some, if not all, of the demands circling in the air. I was carefree and I only participated in situations offering Fragile Love with Glass Affections. I was crushing the Architectural Business World while pursing my own successful part-time Art Design Company. I had an eye for illustrating exactly what customers wanted and I went the extra mile to give it to them. Far from being an average man, I had many accolades hanging on my walls in the office and at home to prove how accomplished I was. I

acknowledged my talent when rendering services to my customers but remained humbled by not bragging to my family and friends. Can Fragile Love with Glass Affections happen to a man like me?

I pulled in front of the logged cabin tucked away deep in the woods where only eight people knew it existed as my car dashboard said it was fifteen minutes after midnight. My homeboys and I bought the getaway spot for moments like that, I guessed. I rushed through the door to find the bar fully stocked. I opened the first bottle of hard liquor I could find and straight to my mouth the bottle went. I hoped the smooth, brown liquor could dull the pain taking over my soul. The conversation with her had me shook as I found myself begging on my knees for hours for her not to leave me. I was sure we could make the situation work for all parties involved except her HUSBAND.

How could every touch, kiss, dance, dinner, or walk in the park be Fragile Love with Glass Affections? She explained her husband was overseas working and the relationship between us meant everything to her. She was lonely and I came into her life at the right time. She wanted to tell me since the night the infamous call showed up on my car's dashboard, but she did not want a tick for tack situation. Her "Girls Trips" were to connect with her husband when she traveled domestically and internationally. How could I have not seen I was being lied to? Fragile Love with Glass Affections is what I do and not what gets done to me. I refused to believe our love was not strong enough to survive.

I fought for our relationship literally on my knees with my arms wrapped around her waist. I am embarrassed of how I tried to stop her from choosing him, her very own husband, over me. If I would have never heard the whispers of her friends, I would be an engaged man enjoying my fiancé somewhere overlooking the perfect beach. I finally faced the fact I was losing the battle of keeping her in my life

and I gave her back her marriage without me. She repeatedly told me she could not continue seeing both of us because things were too deep, and she had to choose her marriage.

I never knew what Fragile Love with Glass Affections felt like or the pain coming with it. I saw my homeboys fall victim to it over and over again from our childhood until now, but never me. The very reason I carried myself with impenetrable walls with no emotions shield me from the pain I was experiencing. She was the first lady I ever gave my heart and Fragile Love with Glass Affections laced with deception and lies caused me to run away from the world. Her vows to another man landed me in a cabin tucked away in the woods where no one could find me. Screaming why without an ear to hear me, I vowed to return to my old ways.

Right then, I took my name out of the pot for love and the happily ever after. I did not need the house on the hill with the picketed fence protecting my son and daughter playing in the yard. Fragile Love with Glass Affections destroyed any future life of the kind My half drunken bottle of liquor and my old lifestyle waited for me to wake up whenever that was. Sleeping off the slumber I put myself in, I woke the next morning with hazy, glazed eyes and wondered exactly where I was before the ache in my heart reminded me of the recent events I wanted to forget.

Guard

Guard your GIFT like your LIFE depends on it because it DOES!

www.ingramcontent.com/pod-product-compliance
Lightning Source LLC
LaVergne TN
LVHW051844080426
835512LV00018B/3068